GIANTS
ARROWS
TARGETS
EAGLES

"Delight yourself also in the Lord, and He shall give you the desires of your heart."
(Psalm 37:4)

Copyright © 2024 Frank Bennett.

The right of Frank Bennett to be identified as the author of this work has been asserted by him in accordance with the Copyright, Designs and Patents Act 1988. All rights reserved. No part of this publication may be reproduced or transmitted in any form or by any means, electronic or mechanical, including photocopy, recording, or any information storage and retrieval system, without permission in writing from the publisher.

Published by Gateway to Destiny
gatewaytodestiny.com
E-mail: contact@gatewaytodestiny.com

ISBN 9798879817188

Acknowledgments:

Editing & design by Al Gibson
Logo design by Brendan Douglas-Henry
Layout and typesetting by Countdown Creative Ltd. countdowncreative.co.uk

A catalogue record for this book is available from the British Library

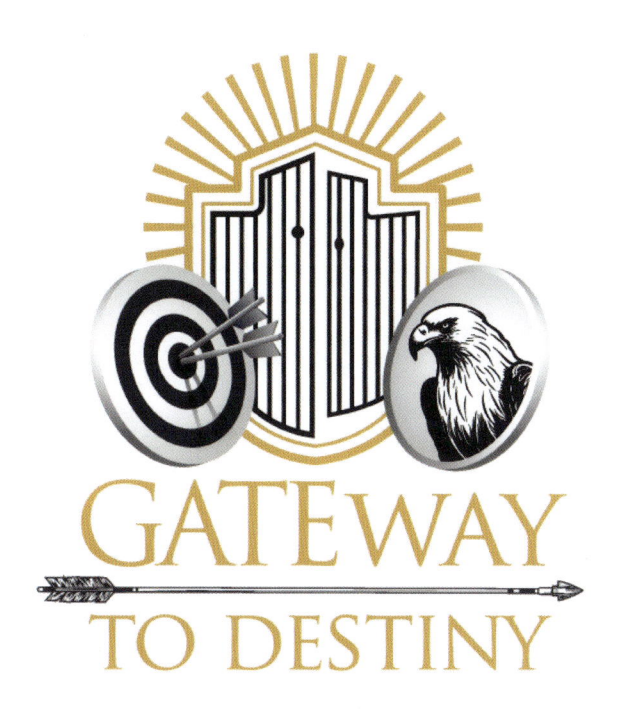

CONTENTS

Introduction	Page 7
4 Important GATEways	Page 10
Making a start	Page 12
Complete your profile	Page 14
GIANTS	Page 17
Identity Scriptures	Page 22
ARROWS	Page 23
TARGETS	Page 33
Whats Sheet	Page 36
Targets – Case Study: Elliott	Page 42
EAGLES	Page 53
Concluding Points	Page 63
Space for further notes	Page 68

About the author: Frank Bennett

The author of GATEway to Destiny and course presenter, Frank Bennett is:

- Part of Crosslink Transformation Network (CTN) which gathers business people together to transform the marketplace. Visit ctnsouthwest.network;
- Lives in Devon in the Southwest of England;
- Former Inspector and Force Training Support Manager with Devon and Cornwall Police;
- A Life Coach who has attended the Gallup USA Faith Strengths Performance Coaching Programme;
- A Leadership and Management Trainer and Training Manager;
- Someone who believes that there is the most fulfilling journey for everyone from Convert to Disciple;
- Visit gatewaytodestiny.com for more information.

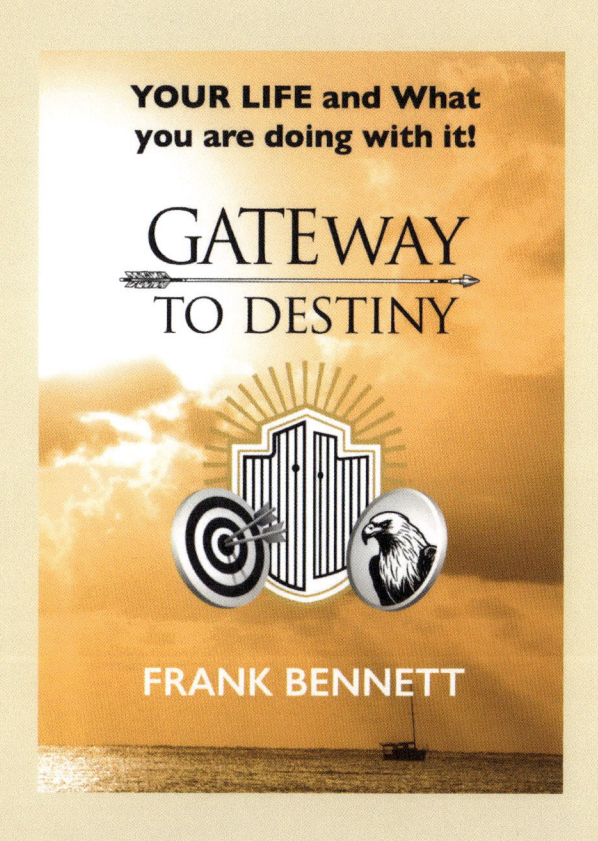

Get the best out of the course

The GATEway to Destiny programme requires your time and commitment in order for you to get the most out of it in terms of your understanding of, and progress towards God's plan and purpose for your life.

As such you need to devote sufficient attention to going through the workbook. Be purposeful and intentional about finding sufficient time to do this, after all you are investing in yourself as you do so.

If you are going through a difficult time emotionally consider waiting until you are in a better frame of mind before starting the course. If you and your partner are both looking to do the programme, it's best you each use your own workbook and complete it individually. This is because your answers to the questions will be very different. You don't want to end up with 'Whats' that are compromises and won't work out for the best in the longer term. You are unique and have been wired to be the way you are and like the things you like. So enjoy the course together in this way, giving each partner the fullest opportunity to express themselves.

It can be really encouraging to work through this programme with others who are keen to also find God's plan and purpose for themselves. So do consider participating in GATEway to Destiny as a house group or as a whole church. It will give everyone a buzz of excitement.

God has a plan and purpose for the unique you and being the loving Father that He is, He writes His plan on your heart.

He gives you the gifts and abilities to achieve the plan with Him. He has set a path before you with the true fulfilment you seek lying alongside that path. It needs a decision of your will to press through the GATEway towards God's plan in order to experience that real fulfilment.

Do you see the gate as shut? A block to progress?
Do you see it as more closed than open? Or more open than closed or fully open?
How you see God will affect how you view your GATEway.

We encourage you to answer God's love and press through your GATEway to the rewards which can only be found beyond.

Introduction and Welcome to the GATEway Programme

Congratulations on coming this far in your journey to discover God's plan and purpose for your life. He made you unique and has equipped you for success! NOW He wants you to achieve all He has put on your heart.

It is no coincidence you are reading this workbook just as it is no coincidence I have written it. God's plan has brought you to read these words just as His plan has inspired me to write them. Together, it is our destiny. But we need to walk through our 'GATEway to Destiny'!

This programme has been designed to help anyone wanting to find God's plan and purpose for their life. It stems from a question I was asked that stopped me in my tracks. The reason being, that I couldn't answer it, even though it was straightforward.

I was with a group of Christians who were looking at the possibility of starting their own businesses. The speaker that evening asked us collectively:

"What has God put the unique you on this earth now to achieve?"

Despite being a Christian for some 18 years, I couldn't answer that question, but it captivated my attention, so there and then I demanded an answer of myself. Five months later I had the answer which comprised of several 'Whats' which I believe God put on my heart.

When I reflected on my journey to that point, I realised it needn't have taken that long and so I devised this programme to help others do so more effectively. Please demand of yourself an answer to that question right now.

"What has God put the unique you on this earth now to achieve?"

GATEway to Destiny is also about you connecting with what God has already put deep inside you, in your very essence, and created you specifically for – your unique purpose! If you are unsure about God having put something deep inside of you then consider this scripture:

> *"You made me from inside out, shaping me in my mother's womb. I praise you for making me in such an awesome and wonderful way. What you do is incredible – I realise this completely! My growing body was not hidden from you as I was formed in secret, as I was intricately put together 'in the depths of the earth.'*
>
> *"You saw me as an embryo, and in your book all my days were written down – the days that were made for me before any of them existed. God your thoughts are so valuable to me! Taken together, they can't be counted!"* (Psalm 139:13-17 FBV)

I invite you to read this scripture again and speak it out believing and accepting that God knows every single thing about you. He knows you so intimately and has created you just as you are and has planned every day of your life for you.

I can state clearly that there is a theme that links together all the Whats God has put on my heart to achieve. This theme is my 'Life Mission'. In my case it is "to help people find their true place in God and to go on to release their full potential in Him and for Him."

There, in twenty-three words, is what I believe my destiny in God to be and today, in writing this workbook and in developing, and presenting this programme I really believe that I am doing a key part of what I have been put on this earth to do. This is a truly fulfilling, exciting and enjoyable, but also a challenging experience.

When I look at my life as an archery target, I know that I am hitting the 'gold centre' when I am involved with this programme. You can have the same sense of fulfilment in your life and hit your life targets.

The 3 Ts

God has given each of us 3 Ts to achieve our life mission. Our 3 Ts are our TIME, TALENT, and TREASURE. I have made a deliberate, active choice to use my 3 Ts to give birth to my Life Mission. You can do the same with your 3 Ts. Would you like to discover your Life Mission by considering the following six steps?

1. Find out what you have been put on this earth to achieve, as a unique individual;

2. Have insight into whether you have a five-fold ministry; Could you be an Apostle, Prophet, Pastor, Evangelist, or Teacher?

3. Know your spiritual giftings and how this influences your Whats;

4. Determine how positive and negative experiences in your life can influence the Whats God has put on your heart to achieve;

5. Consider how your personality can help your success rather than hinder it; and

6. Be assured as to how you can overcome the Giants who seek to prevent you from reaching your full potential in God.

If you would like to consider any or all of these steps, then this programme is for you.
I wish you every success and can tell you that the GATEway is open, if you will but accept and walk through it.

4 Important GATEways

GATEways are something we need to walk through along the path of our life journey. If you are stopped by a gate, you may never actually get to your destination. Here, GATE stands for Giants, Arrows, Targets and Eagles and each section is important individually and can help you, not just find God's plan and purpose for your life, but also achieve your FULL potential in God.

GIANTS

The Giants Section comes from my life experience as the designer of this programme which has led me to the realisation that Giants have to be dealt with throughout the whole course of one's life journey.

Giants can try to stop us from starting, stop or delay our progress, or divert us along unproductive paths. They can come in many different guises, but we have to recognise and deal with them, in order to be really successful rather than just average. God has equipped each of us to achieve our full potential. We are wired for excellence.

ARROWS

The Arrows Section is inspired by Isaiah 49:1-2 which says:

"God has made me a polished arrow."

If we do not realise and fully accept that we are a weapon in God's hand we can easily be prevented from realising our true worth, effectiveness and destiny. Understanding and accepting our identity in God is the foundation on which we will build. As part of this programme, we will look at the key aspects of our spirit, will, mind and emotions as well as our security, acceptance and significance.

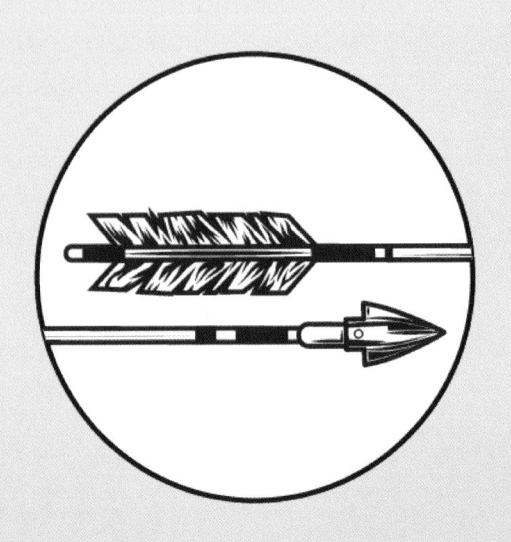

GATEWAY TO DESTINY

TARGETS

The Targets Section is where we will begin to look at our dreams and aspirations in God so that we can identify our Whats. These are the things God has put on our heart to connect with and to achieve. We will then prioritise our Whats so we are clear which are the most important.

We will also examine how our spiritual giftings, personality and our positive or negative experiences might influence our Whats and how they might help us best achieve them. We will list our Whats in a way that ensures we know them clearly and unambiguously and can take steps to begin to achieve them in line with how God has created us.

One of the real barriers to achieving the things God has put on our heart to do is that we don't know where to start. By being really clear on our Whats we can identify and take steps to bring each of them to life actively and not passively.

This programme is specifically designed to allow YOU to actually start taking steps to achieve YOUR dreams and aspirations. It is definitely not a theory-only programme.

EAGLES

Standing strong then Flying High! The Eagles Section is all about the attitudes and habits we need to progress from average to excellent; from convert to disciple.

A key part is the all-important proactive choices we need to make to overcome self-limiting thoughts and beliefs. We need to examine what we need to do to soar like an eagle whilst developing the resilience to stand strong in our identity in Christ and in the knowledge of who God is.

There is a clear link between your perception of your life, what you subsequently do and the ultimate results you get. This section is designed to help you focus on moving from recognition and acceptance of who you are in God to developing and excelling in all that God wants you to be. So you can make a Kingdom impact with the precious life God has given you

It is very much about making the journey from convert to disciple. A Christian disciple is someone who sets out to make God's will the most important part of their life and see themselves as a steward of, rather than an owner of, the life God has blessed them with.

MAKING A START

Only you can walk through the GATEway to your Destiny and go on to accomplish the things you have been put on this earth to achieve.

You already know in your life experiences to date, that real success takes great energy and effort and to be successful over a long period takes resilience and focus as well.

So I am going to list some of the things which I know can hinder us from achieving God's best for our life. Some may apply to you more than others but before doing that I want to set out what I feel is a useful framework for the development of a ministry, your ministry, although it can also apply equally to the start and development of a business.

STEP 1. DREAM

Before we can develop and progress the plans God has for us we need to dream to allow God to move in a way that shows us what the future might hold. Dreams can motivate and guide us well if they are of God. They can also distract us if they are not from God and lead us to waste our 3 Ts.

STEP 2. DARE

Dreaming is wonderful, it is creative and can be really inspirational, but dreams need to be turned into reality as, without application, they remain just daydreams. You will need to start taking some initial steps such as talking to other people who you know and trust about your dreams. Putting some Time, Talent and Treasure into looking at doing some of the things necessary to investigate the possibilities. This is the start of daring to take action.

STEP 3. CREATE

Here you have dreamed the dreams, looked at them from many angles and now begin to take real and actual steps to bring them to birth. Even now some of the key things God has put on your heart may be coming to mind and you have an excitement about them every time your mind goes back to them.

You will, in this stage, be actually committing your Time, Talent and Treasure to your dreams. Creating always costs. At this point you have a real emotional as well as any other investment in your dreams. So, believing it is God's dreams that you are partnering with is really important. But how do you know with 100% certainty that they are God-given?

The answer is, you don't. It is a step of faith, but if what God has put on your heart lines up with the giftings and abilities He has given you, and works with your personality not against it, and is propelled by some of your life experiences whether positive or negative, then at least you can have greater confidence they just might be from God and are worth pursuing. You can then take Godly advice and counsel and move forward but ultimately it is between you and God.

STEP 4. GROW

Once something, and in this case your dream, has been dreamt, you have dared and now created, then for it to become everything it could be you might well need to grow it further. Take additional steps to increase it further. Again, your 3 Ts will be involved and positive action needed and taken.

STEP 5. EXPAND

This step is to maximise all that your dreams could be and to reach their full potential. It is important to know the extent of your dreams so that you do not under develop them or take them further than God intends.

But you might be thinking, "I don't have a huge ministry, there are just a few things I believe God has put on my heart to do". That's fine. Each of us become 'good and faithful servants' by doing what God has given us to do and by living the unique life He has given us. Knowing what God has put on our heart, knowing the dreams He has given you are the start of that. We are never in competition with other people. We are unique.

Each of these five steps builds one on the other; they are foundational to each other. We know God wants us to achieve all that He has for us. If God has given you dreams, He is big enough to achieve them but the journey to the place of real achievement will both test and develop your relationship with Him. In progressing through to the achievement of your dreams you will really discover the answer to two vital questions of identity.

1. Who you are in God; and

2. Who you really say God is, but more about that later.

At this point what does the gate in front of you look like? Do you believe the GATEway to your Destiny is open or closed? I invite you to see and believe that it is open and that you can walk through it on a journey of adventure and fulfilment with God and in doing so make the journey from Convert to Disciple if you haven't done so already.

Go on, give that gate a push now to open it wide. If it has rusted over the years give it a really good kick being assured it will open, not just because of you but because of Him.

Complete your profile

As part of your GATEway to Destiny experience, you will find it helpful to take a couple of online assessments and complete the Profile Sheet on the right.

1. MY SPIRITUAL GIFTS - fivefoldsurvey.com

There are many Spiritual Gift Assessments available online that will assist you to get a more rounded understanding of your unique self. However, not all provide clear and easily understandable results. One I have found that does is fivefoldsurvey.com. Take the free online assessment made available by Mike Breen which will provide you with some valuable insights which you can include in your Profile Sheet. This is the area of the 5-fold ministry graces of Apostles, Prophets, Evangelists, Pastors and Teachers as per Ephesians 4:11. (Please note the distinction made between base and phase in the information provided with your results.)

2. MY PERSONALITY

This section is for you to note down key aspects of your personality. This is of importance as our personality determines a great deal, not so much about what we like to do, but in the way we like to do it. For example, if you are task-focused and structured, task/structured means you like getting a job done, you prefer an agenda, you are focused on results and you appreciate clear direction. So, if you work in another way, you cause yourself tension and frustration.

By knowing your preferences and recognising they are God-given you can help yourself to be the best you can be. Managers can spend so much time trying to solve staff issues when in essence they are personality issues. Christians have an advantage here when we recognise, value, and seek to maximise the benefits of our personality. By recognising that our personality is God-given, we can accept that God has given others their personality just as He intended. So, rather than fighting against their personality we can seek to work with them knowing God has made that unique person, just as He has made the unique you.

There are many personality type assessments available, and some are more helpful than others. One of those I found to be simple but very useful and would recommend is on pages 106-111 of the book *Network Participants Guide Revised* by Bruce Bugbee, Don Cousins with Wendy Seidman, published by Harper Collins. Copyright prohibits me from including it here. This assessment asks you a small number of questions which show how you are both energised and motivated. Depending on your answers you can then reveal whether you are people or task oriented as well as whether you are structured or unstructured in personality. You then get an explanation of what each type means and how you prefer to work. This is of great use when you start to define your Whats in more detail as per the Targets Section.

PROFILE SHEET

MY SPIRITUAL GIFTS
Circle any ministry giftings relevant to you following your 5-fold Assessment:

APOSTLE   PROPHET   EVANGELIST   PASTOR   TEACHER

MY PERSONALITY
Enter the results from your personality assessment(s)

List some of your positive Life Experiences (See page 16)

List some of your negative Life Experiences (See page 16)

MY POSITIVE & NEGATIVE LIFE EXERIENCES

This section of the Profile Sheet reflects the impact our key experiences of life have had on us to date in motivating us to do our Whats. Write down any major experiences you have had in life both positive and negative.

For example, as a 20-year-old Police Officer, it was my job to inform next of kin that a husband, wife, mother, father, son, or a daughter had died suddenly and weren't coming home. This was a major experience for me as a young man which is still very relevant for me today.

It brought me face to face with the realisation that "Life is a privilege, not a right and that none of us are guaranteed tomorrow." This is still very much a major personal driver for me in wanting to help people make the very best of the great privilege that is our life and to personalise that, your life.

So, please list some of your life experiences in the Profile Sheet that are the key influencers to you both positively and negatively. The benefit of doing this will become clearer when you have read our case study later.

Something for you to be aware of is that when you begin to really seek to become aware of your deepest desires in God the waters sometimes seem to get muddier. And it almost seems harder to define those deepest desires clearly. This is perfectly normal, and so give yourself permission to feel that way if it happens. The waters will clear up as the programme progresses and we start to see how it might all fit together.

GIANTS

We will refer to Giants throughout this programme. It is how big you perceive them to be that will determine how much of a hold they have over you and your life. And it is how big you believe God is in relation to the Giants that will determine your level of success in overcoming them.

As we have already discovered, Giants will generally:

- Stop you from starting;
- Slow you down;
- Stop your progress if you have already started; or
- Divert you from a productive path to an unproductive one.

This workbook is designed to help you work through and identify YOUR dreams in God and plan a course of action where you can start taking some initial steps. The programme can also point out the attitudes, behaviours and habits you need to succeed. We aim to help you take these three steps:

1. Dream;
2. Dare; and
3. Create.

These will point you in the right direction for Steps 4 and 5.

The purpose of dreaming in God is to allow Him to share with us the things that are on our hearts as well as on His. God may have already put things deep within you which He wants you to achieve, and some of the scriptures we cover in the Arrows Section will help with that.

If we do not overcome passivity and take positive action, we let our dreams get covered up by the other aspects of daily living; like a valuable item that has been put in a cupboard, covered up and lost from sight. Dreaming also connects us emotionally with the things He has put on our hearts. God has given emotions to men and women. What is valuable to you might well not be so valuable to me and vice-versa, but what God has put on your heart is valuable to you AND to God and that is all that matters.

If you can be prevented from dreaming, slowed down, or diverted from it, what are the potential consequences? Write them down in the space below:

....
....
....
....
....

You have already overcome some Giants in your life. Awareness of your Giants and tactics to reduce or avoid their impact are of great benefit. Write them down in the space below:

1. What are the things that may prevent you from dreaming about what God has put on your heart?

....
....
....
....
....
....

2. Looking at each in turn, write down what you can do to prevent or minimise the potential hindrance caused by each. Spend some time on this, don't skip over it!

....
....
....
....
....
....

Some of the things which have potentially prevented me from dreaming are:

- Not believing that I am worthy to have any Godly dreams or aspirations.
- Other people in my life believing and saying that I cannot achieve anything.
- Having seemingly had a dream in the past which has not come to fruition.
- Believing that I don't have the talent or gifting to carry through things I believe are God-given.
- Not believing that God speaks to ME.
- Believing that as I don't have the resources, including the time to achieve my dreams it is pointless me dreaming anyway.
- I have to put food on the table now so I can't afford to dream, after all, what is the point?
- I might fail so it is better not to try.
- I just can't get clear in my dreams; it all seems like a fog, so many ideas, where do I start?
- Other people need my time, talent and treasure, it would be selfish to spend time dreaming.
- I am too old to dream; it is too late in life for me, or
- I am too young to dream; I have plenty of time later in life to dream.

You will probably have other potential barriers. It is important that you realise we do not all have the same barriers, although there are some that are more prevalent than others.

Self-doubt is very common. That is why our identity in God is so important and you can overcome this Giant by not just reading the scriptures in the Arrows Section but by ACCEPTING them and APPLYING them to your life. This is the start of learning to stand strong in God and where you develop a clear understanding for yourself of who you say He is.

Fear of failure is a barrier that is often accompanied by fear of looking foolish in the eyes of others. Putting God's plan and purpose for your life ahead of your own fears helps. This involves controlling your emotions through God's Word and use of your will in making positive decisions.

Lack of clarity is also a great hindrance. Having no real clear focus on what your dreams are and not being able to separate each from the other can prevent you from identifying steps which can bring your dreams to fruition. Applying focus can really help here. Focus is just what completing this programme can bring. Please see it through and write your answers down. Just writing things down can really help get the fog of confusion out of your mind and that is a real step forward to clarity and success.

Age, either too young or old frequently comes up. Don't believe this lie. God has created you unique. You were born for NOW. As long as you have breath your dreams live because you do.

Lack of time and or other resources are potential barriers but please note that it is NEVER 'not having time' that is the barrier. There are twenty-four hours in everyone's day. The barrier is how we use our time and how we prioritise it or fail to prioritise it.

Write down below what might prevent you from completing this programme.

....
....
....
....
....
....
....

Now, write down what you WILL DO NOW to prevent those things from hindering your completion of this programme. After all, what is more important in your life than finding God's plan and purpose for your unique life and living it out as God intends?

....
....
....
....
....
....
....
....

The key way to defeat a Giant is to confront the thoughts it brings to your mind with what God's Word says. Giants want you to believe they are big and strong as they want to intimidate you, to make you afraid. Giants seek to bring doubt and fear to your mind by stirring up negative emotions within you.

But remember what David did to Goliath. Why was David not intimidated by this Giant? Read it for yourself in 1 Samuel Chapter 17. Here you will see how David believed in God and when you compare a Giant to God, as David did, then there is no contest. No Giant can stand against God. David applied his knowledge of his God to his situation and circumstances.

He controlled his emotions directly by making his mind focus on how big God is, not how big the Giant was. He then used his will to decide what he should do, run or fight, and he chose to take a risk and fight. He already knew how God had kept him and protected him in situations earlier in his life. In short, David understood this vital point; his identity in God. God has kept you through situations earlier in your life. So are you prepared to fight the enemy Giants that seek to intimidate you and stop you fulfilling your God-given purpose?

When David killed the Giant the whole of Israel benefited. When you defeat your Giants and achieve your God-given dreams many others will benefit. All those who you will reach and help by achieving God's plan for your life need you to fight for your dreams. Remember, this is not just all about you. It is about God's plan for OTHERS being outworked through you and with you. This is one of the pivotal moments and so it is also a good time to pray. Please read this next piece of text as a prayer but also as a declaration. Read it and declare it aloud.

GATEway TO DESTINY

Prayer of Commitment

Heavenly Father, I thank you that you love me and I thank you for loving me so much that you gave your only Son, my Lord Jesus Christ, to die for me and to take away my sins. I realise that you also love all of mankind, every man, woman, and child. I thank you that you do not want any of them to be separated from you in eternity and that you have a plan and purpose for my life in bringing your love to others.

I acknowledge that you have created me unique. I acknowledge that I am not an accident or a mistake, but I am your child. I am wanted and accepted and have a vital part to play in your plan. I want to be a disciple not just a convert.

I accept responsibility for the life you have given me to be a steward of. I determine that I will live this life for your glory and that I will not turn back from achieving the life purpose you have given me. I will not be intimidated or robbed of my destiny in you.

Please help me really understand what you have put on my heart to achieve. Help me through your Holy Spirit to understand that this, my life, is not all about me. It is about showing Your great love to those who you want to reach through me.

I give the unique person you have made me to be, to you. I accept who you have made me to be, and I willingly accept the commission you have given to me. I will not turn back. I am fully yours now and forever.

Signed: ………………………… Date: …………………………

Now, if you really mean this, sign your name above as a mark of your commitment and intention to serve God out of gratitude for what He has done for you out of His great love.

Just as it was for David, so it is important for you to understand and accept your identity in God. This is a fitting point on which to move on to the next section, Arrows. This understanding is so foundational it is worth spending time on. It must be a solid, concrete foundation so that it can genuinely support and sustain all that God wants to do in you and through you. So, let's take the next step on the journey.

IDENTITY SCRIPTURES –
This is what God says about me

VERSE	POINT	YES	NO	UNSURE
Psalm 139:1	**God knows me personally.**			
Psalm 139:4	**He knows my thoughts.**			
Psalm 139:13-14	**God created me I'm wonderfully made.**			
Psalm 139:16	**He has ordained every day of my life.**			
John 1:2	**I am a child of God.**			
John 15:15-16	**Jesus says I am a friend.**			
Romans 8:14	**I am a son / daughter of God.**			
Romans 8:17	**I am an Heir of God - Inheritance.**			
1 Corinthians 3:16	**God's Spirit lives in me.**			
1 Corinthians 12:27	**I am part of Christ's Body.**			
2 Corinthians 5:17	**I am a new creation.**			
Ephesians 2:10	**I am God's workmanship.**			
1 Peter 5:8	**I am an enemy of the devil.**			
Isaiah 49:1-2	**God created me, a weapon.**			

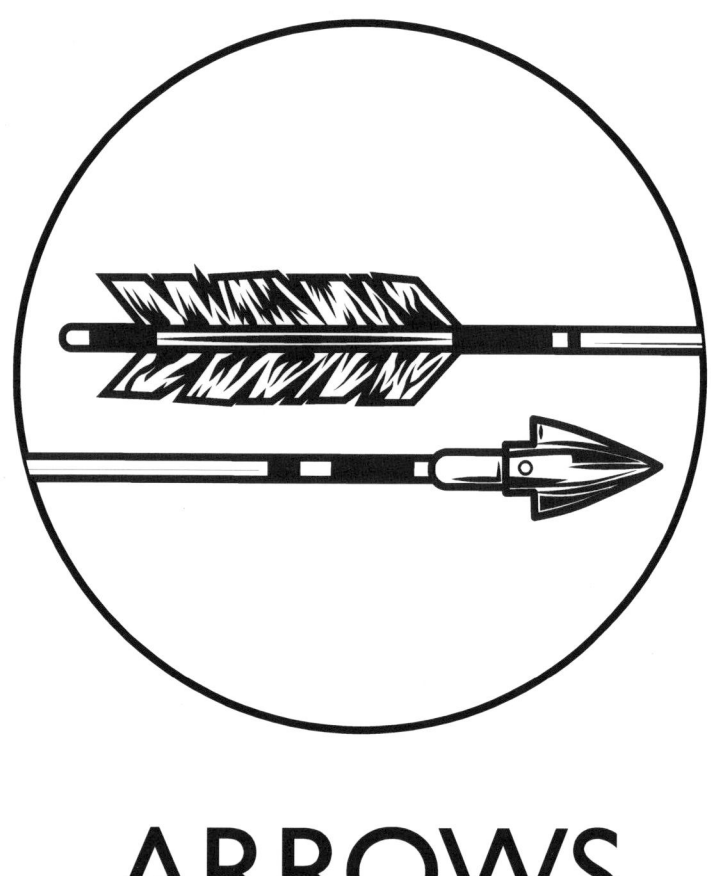

ARROWS

In the adjacent table of Identity Scriptures you will find verses from the Bible that describe a relevant facet of your life. Read each of them carefully and evaluate your thinking about each one. Add a tick in the relevant column, yes if you agree, no if you disagree and unsure if you are unable to answer.

Please don't just automatically tick each one as yes because you know that these are verses from the Bible. Read each one carefully to see whether you agree with the point being made. Take this a stage further by, before ticking, asking yourself what evidence is there in your life to support where you are placing this tick? Would others who know you well be able to state that, from what they see, there is sufficient evidence to indicate you believe each point?

Once you have completed this read each line another time. This time, tick the relevant column for whether YOU believe this APPLIES TO YOU PERSONALLY. Why do you need to do this a second time? The answer is because, unless you believe each point applies to YOU, you will not be able to stand on it when your Giants stand up to intimidate you. Your Giants will do just that. If you are not settled and determined in yourself about your identity in Christ, you will find it hard to stand and overcome that intimidation as your concrete foundation will be cracked.

The Bible tells us in James 1:8, that we should not be 'double-minded'. We need to be of one mind, that is, without doubt, about who we are in God. Even Jesus resisted the devil with "It is written." It is the same for us. We will overcome by knowing what "is written" about us AND accepting it personally.

This section is called 'Arrows' because we have been created as a weapon in God's hand. In one of the comments about Jesus in 1 John 3:8 it says, *"the Son of God came for this purpose: to destroy the devil's work."* Jesus gave His disciples the Great Commission, to go into all the world and make disciples of all nations (Matthew 28:19-20). When we make disciples, we are destroying the works of the devil and he doesn't like that.

Jot down in the space below what effect it would have on your aspirations and dreams in God if the devil could successfully convince you that you are not a weapon at all.

....
....
....
....
....
....
....
....
....
....

If you look at the arrow below, you will see that it has three main parts: the head, the shaft and the flights. Let's look at each in turn, review each part and illustrate how we can see ourselves as an Arrow.

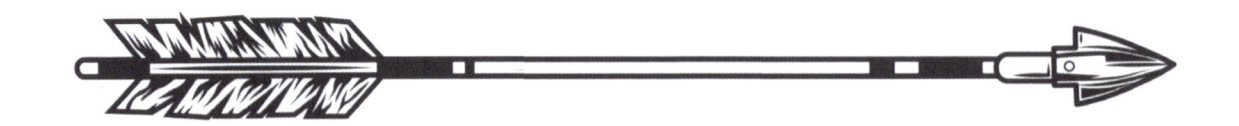

In Old Testament times arrows were one of the main long-distance weapons and all Israel's soldiers would be familiar with the weapon. They would certainly know a good arrow from a poor one. Arrows were made for hunting, target practice or for warfare. Those who made arrows would carefully select the materials so that maximum accuracy could be achieved. Let's look at each part of the arrow specifically.

THE ARROW HEAD

The Head was the piece which did the damage; the section that made the impact. It had to be sharp but also streamlined to travel through the air as well as hard enough to withstand contact with the target. The rest of the arrow is there to get the impact making section to the target.

You and I make the maximum impact when God gets our spiritual gifting and our natural abilities dead centre in the target. God has made you with both of these elements together in the single person you are. After all, God is God and He could have made you any way He wanted, and I would like you to accept that He has done just that.

He has made you just as He wanted, with a unique combination of spiritual gifts and natural abilities. As such, will you now accept that you are a weapon in God's hand and really value the spiritual giftings and natural abilities He has given you?

In the space below write a declaration about how you see yourself, about the importance of your Arrowhead giftings and abilities and the impact you can make through God.

....
....
....
....
....
....
....

THE ARROW SHAFT

The Shaft is the most sizeable section and joins the impact-making head to the direction-giving flights. The Shaft was made from wood and skilled arrow-makers chose pieces of wood which they cut and shaped to the best length and diameter. All the knobbles and bobbles were removed to give true flight. The Shaft also had to be securely fastened to the Head and Flights, as the Shaft had to withstand the powerful forces of being released from the bow and of hitting the target. It must get the head to its destination.

The Shaft can represent our character. We need Godly character as well as impact-making giftings and abilities. Just in case you do not see the value of character, stop to think about high profile Christians with large well-known ministries who have had to give them up due to errors of judgement and personal failures. We are all human and so have weaknesses and can easily fall unless we guard our character closely and wisely whilst resisting temptation. I never said this would be easy, it isn't, but it is so worthwhile.

People will accept us into their situations depending on what they see of us. Our character is shown to others largely through what we do with our mind, will and emotions. The Bible tells us that we are spiritual beings temporarily resident in a human body. Our spirit is eternal and will live on after our body dies. Our body contains our mind, will and emotions. That is how God created us – with all these parts. He didn't need to give us emotions, but He did hence others see of us what we make of our mind, will and emotions.

We use our mind to think and reason and our emotions can line up with our mind or contradict it. Going back to David overcoming Goliath, David might have had some fears, but he used his mind actively. He was not passive or submissive in his thinking. He used all he knew of God's nature and provision by bringing them to mind and so could hold any fears in check with those positive thoughts about God.

He seemed to have other emotions such as indignation that this Goliath could taunt God's Chosen People so he harnessed this emotion to drive him on to stand and fight. But he still had a decision to make when he chose to fight or not. David chose to fight. He felt his emotions, thought his thoughts, but then made a decision to fight. Decision making is the function of our will. Some people such as polar explorers and top performing sports stars are strong willed. They choose to train and compete enduring the physical and mental pain they have to overcome to be the best.

It is the same with high-performing Christians. Each of us is the same and we make decisions through our will in one of two ways. One way is by positive choice – being assertive and taking responsibility. Our will is active. Secondly by passivity – not being assertive and not taking positive decisions but opting out. Either way it is a decision.

The same applies to finding God's plan for your life. At the moment you have chosen positively to do something to progress this, although that could turn to passivity in the future. It is up to you; it is a choice of your will. Guard your character as it is so important in getting your arrowhead to its target. Recognise and accept you have a mind, emotions and a will and use them deliberately and actively. Become an Overcomer.

THE ARROW FLIGHTS

The Flights are there to enable our arrows to fly well through the air and maximise accuracy. Flights can affect accuracy positively or negatively and influence both direction and elevation. Without Flights an arrow is a pointed stick. It is still dangerous, but not nearly as dangerous as it could be. Which would you most fear, the pointed stick, or the arrow?

GATEway
TO DESTINY

For Christians, our difference is our connection with our God. It is God who has created us and who has the plan and purpose for our life. His plan, the outworking of which brings our deepest sense of fulfilment and joy.

God knows our impact making potential and wants to develop our character. He needs us to listen to Him and allow ourselves to be fired through the air from His bow towards the centre of the target which is His plan for us. We must be sensitive enough to hear and obedient enough to follow, to allow Him to fire us forward.

The important point here is whose you say you are. If you believe your life is your own to do what you want with, you will use your 3 Ts just as you want to. If you believe Jesus is your Lord and you are submitted to God through Him then you see yourself as a steward of your life, not as an owner, and you will want to use your 3 Ts in line with His purposes. But you will have to make those positive, assertive decisions of your will to be effective.

On a scale of 1 to 10 where 1 is 'I am totally my own' and 10 is 'I am totally God's', where do you find yourself? Consider the actual evidence to back this up before placing an X.

> 1 > 2 > 3 > 4 > 5 > 6 > 7 > 8 > 9 > 10 >

Now, in the space below, write down what the implications are for you achieving God's plan and purpose for your life based on where on the scale you have marked your X.

....
....
....
....
....
....
....

Now, decide on the scale where you really want to mark your X. If there is a difference between your placements of the two marks, in the space below write down how YOU will get to the second X and what YOU will actually DO to get to where you want to be.

....
....
....
....
....

GATEWAY TO DESTINY

PROGRESS CHECK

This will help you check your understanding of the programme so far and will help to cement your learning and progress. Please spend a few moments to answer the questions below in your own words.

1. What does the Arrowhead represent in your life?

....
....
....
....

2. What does the Shaft represent in your life?

....
....
....
....

3. What do the Flights represent in your life?

....
....
....
....

4. What are the 3 Ts?

They are my: T...................... T .... and T........................

5. If you signed the declaration, did you do so willingly out of heartfelt gratitude, or did it seem like something you ought to do out of duty?

....
....
....
....
....

6. Action point – in the next twenty-four hours, will you tell someone that you have made this declaration and explain why and what it means to you personally? Use the space below to help you draft out the key points of what you might say.

....
....
....
....

The last part of this Arrows Section relates to two other aspects of your identity as a Christian as they shape how you think and feel about yourself and to withstand your Giants you will need to recognise these points and be assured of your answers.

POSITION VS PERFORMANCE

This point deals with who we are in Christ and also the level of what we do. The Bible teaches us that when we accept Jesus as our Saviour, we become children of God. We cannot earn our salvation by good works, which is, doing things for God. It is our past sins that separate us from God, and it is only through accepting Jesus as our saviour that our past sins are dealt with (John 3:16) and we are given eternal life.

So, you need to be clear on this, that doing the things God has put on your heart to do will not gain you salvation, as that has come through Jesus. Your position is not dependent on your performance. Be clear on this rejoicing in the position you have gained through the death and resurrection of Jesus. So, does that mean your performance is irrelevant and you can sit back, put my feet up and passively while your life away month by month and year by year?

Absolutely not, is the answer. Read the Parables of the Talents and the Wise and Foolish Virgins in Matthew 25:1-30. God wants you to make the best of the unique package of gifts and abilities which make up the unique you. He wants a return from all of us but this should not be out of a sense of duty but should flow out of us with a real sense of joy and gratitude. If you don't feel that gratitude, read over the Crucifixion passages in Mark Chapter 15 and write a short letter to Jesus below to tell Him what you think of what He has done for you.

Dear Jesus
....
....
....
....
....
....
....
....

Your performance will not affect your position, but it will directly affect your enjoyment of your life and the fulfilment you seek. Each of us would like to feel truly fulfilled in our life. This true fulfilment is only found in serving others through the unique persons we have been created to be. That's why this course can never be just about you; it must always be about how you help others in line with God's plan for your life.

All the great men and women of the Bible led lives which affected others, and many paid the ultimate price. It was never just about them. We should not and cannot walk by on the other side of the road just because it isn't our gifting. We all need to be first aiders for the lost and hurting but we will maximise our performance by understanding the gifts and natural abilities we have been given and working with them to make maximum impact with our Arrowhead.

Some Giants might try to intimidate you by telling you that your performance is and never will be good enough for God. This is a lie. Do not believe it. Resist it with "It is written…" and quote John 3:16 and then give thanks that your position is assured just by you having accepted Jesus. Then tell your Giant that you thank it for motivating you to fully achieve God's plan for your life; after a while it will leave you alone.

SECURITY, ACCEPTANCE & SIGNIFICANCE

These are three common factors which can either negatively or positively affect your view of yourself. Therefore, these can potentially affect your mind and emotions, which in turn through your will, determine your behaviour.

SECURITY

Your sense of personal security as a human being is a big factor in your life whether you realise it or not.

If you look for your sense of security in any of the things listed below, what happens when they are no longer in place?

- Your husband / wife / boyfriend / girlfriend;
- Your job / income;
- Your ownership of your own home; and
- Your health.

Unless your sense of security comes from your personal relationship with God then the moment any of the above or your other security props are even threatened, your mind and emotions can become troubled, and you can become fearful. When your security is shaken the tendency is to hide away, which will stop you in pursuing and fulfilling God's plan for your life.

Take a few moments to ask God if you are putting your security in anyone or anything other than Him and resolve to understand that your security is in Him alone. Remember Job in the Bible who lost everything he had, yet still refused to do anything other than remain in relationship with God. You will need this understanding of your security, stickability and resilience so that when Giants of circumstances come against you, you can still press on deeper into God's plan.

ACCEPTANCE

Again, this is a real identity feature for many people. Being and wanting to feel accepted by others is part of human nature. But if we look for acceptance in others rather than in God we are always a wrong word or look away from being unsettled.

Many of us can remember cruel words spoken to us in the playground by other children, or later in life by adults, some of whom we thought liked or loved us. Each of us has done something we are not proud of in our life, but our real acceptance is only found in God.

How do I know you are accepted? The answer is in John 3:16 because Jesus died for you. Regardless of whatever horrible things others may have said about us, we can stand resolute with a sense of inner joy and peace, knowing that we are accepted not just for now but for all eternity.

So when people say "You will never achieve God's plan, God doesn't love you," you can stand knowing "It is written" and written in blood that He does love you and accepts you. That doesn't mean we should be rude and unhelpful to others; rather it means we can stand despite what others may say just like Job did. Just like the disciples did. Just like many other Christians you know did and do every day.

Accepting God loves you really does help you with your confidence to believe that you are hearing from God in the Whats you believe He has put on your heart. It also helps you in really accepting the gifts and abilities He has given you and in stepping out to try things with them knowing that if you get things wrong God still accepts you. This is priceless because you are priceless.

SIGNIFICANCE

I can, and I am sure you can also, think of people you know who are seemingly always trying hard to please other people and who always seem to be unhappy unless they receive affirmation from someone else. An example is a child striving and competing to be more successful than their brother / sister in the eyes of a parent.

If you turn to other people or other things to boost your sense of significance, you will always be constantly disappointed. Do you need the latest gadget, the latest make up or fashion, the biggest car, the most expensive house before you feel significant? Understanding that we really are significant in God's eyes gives us the freedom to be who we really are. You, having the confidence to believe that you are significant means that you do not have to prove it to anyone.

My significance is proven by the price God has paid for me through Jesus. I just have to accept it. I do not have to compete with others.

Even when I am achieving God's plan for my life by doing great things which other people never even see I am still significant, and I can rejoice. Yes, it is great when others speak about me in a way which makes me feel significant, but my world does not come crashing down because nobody says anything positive about me. Understanding this can help you to overcome this Giant.

If your life is an Arrow, a very real, powerful, and unique weapon in God's hand, have you been hitting your life targets? Look at the archery target below and imagine that the target represents God's plan for your life then ask yourself the question

Where have my arrows been hitting up until now? Are there any in the gold centre, in the red, blue, black or white areas? Have I hit the target at all?

What difference will it make to me if I never actually hit the gold centre of my life targets?

This Arrows Section is intended to enable you to understand, but more than this to ACCEPT, that you are a weapon in God's hand. I hope it has helped you see that your mind, will, emotions, natural abilities, spiritual giftings, sensitivity and obedience to God are valuable tools which need to be held in the highest regard and actually used. An Arrow needs a target. God wants to fire the unique you at specific situations where you can make a real impact. This leads us to the next section, Targets, where you can focus on what God has for you to achieve in your life right now.

TARGETS

In this section you can begin to focus on your Whats. These are the things God has put on your heart to achieve in your time on earth and with the 3 Ts He has given you.

To do this fully you need to have confidence that:

- God has spoken to you, speaks to you now and will continue to speak to you in the future about your aspirations and dreams in God;
- He has given you spiritual gifting;
- He has given you natural abilities;
- Your unique personality shapes the way you can best achieve your Whats;
- God has already been shaping and equipping you through your life experiences for the achievement of your God-given aspirations and dreams and;
- No matter whether some are large or small dreams, if you are partnering with God, you can have hope that they will come about.

But what if I make a mistake? What if this is just wishful thinking and it is not really from God? Then at least you will have tried. At least you will be able to say, "I gave it my best shot" and you won't be looking back on your life in a few years' time with regrets. Stepping out into Godly dreams will take your relationship with God to another level.

Let's get started. Two blank Whats Sheets follow on pages 36 and 37 and each row is numbered from one to twelve. For the moment, ignore the Gold, Red etc. columns on the right. We will return to them later as they do play a vital part.

On your Whats Sheet, start to write down those things which you believe God has put on your heart to do with your life which involves helping other people or the setting up of things to help other people. Importantly please separate your Whats so that only one is contained in each row.

Please DO NOT:

- Filter anything out at all. You have a green light to put anything down if you think it might just be from God. You can always delete it later if necessary;

- Consider resources at this time, even if you can never see yourself having the resources to achieve the What, still write it down. Don't rob yourself or limit yourself;

- It's important to be able to separate each What from each other as each one will require separate action from you; and

- Don't be too concerned if you cannot describe the What accurately, just write down the gist of it, especially the VERBS which describe what you will actually DO.

Please DO:

- Seek God and ask Him to reveal to you everything that He has for you. Tell Him that you want to put His will first;

- Thank Him for His love for you and in advance for speaking to you about the plans He has for you and for the lives of other people He wants to impact through and with you; and

- Guard your time for this process wisely. This is an important time. You will need to prioritise your time and if necessary, postpone undertaking some less important things.

STARTING OFF – SOME HELPFUL TIPS

Some people can start filling in their Whats Sheets seemingly quickly, but that does not apply to everyone. So, some tips and then some trigger questions might help you. They helped me.

- If things don't come to mind easily, try initially to visualise your thoughts. See yourself doing whatever your heart's desire is and then write that down even if you only have the gist of it.

- Some people respond quickly to situations that grab their emotions. So identify when you are most emotionally connected to people and / or the situations and describe what you are doing and how your emotions are harnessed.

- Some people respond to hearing, so listen for God's voice. Close your eyes to avoid distractions.

- Keep a pad and pen with you over the next few weeks, even by the bedside, as God does speak to some of us through our actual dreams to influence our inspirational dreams.

- Set aside a specific time each day to devote to just seeking God for your Whats, make that time. You will be glad you did.

- Push yourself to think really deeply and review your list several times. It can be hard work to think so deeply but persevere. Do not accept poor levels of thought from yourself. Use your will to drive you to think deeply.

SOME TRIGGER QUESTIONS

To help identify your Whats, ask yourself each question in turn and listen for the responses you receive:

- You get a word from God that your dreams are going to come true. So what will come true?

- Things which have been on my heart for some time and which don't seem to go away are………………......?

- I am most happy when I am doing ……………….... for others.

- I am most on purpose when…………………......?

- I am most fulfilled when …………………......?

- What words come to mind when I think of my life purpose?

- Part of my life purpose is …………………......?

- If I could only achieve one thing in the rest of my life, what would it be?

- Visualise yourself as an Arrow and that God has you in His Bow. You are going to hit the gold centre of your Target. What situations is God firing you into to make the maximum impact…………………......?

- What angers you most in the world?

- What value would you defend to the death?

- Thinking back to your positive and negative experiences in life what is God saying to you about them?

WHATS SHEET

No		Gold	Red	Blue	Black	White
1						
2						
3						
4						
5						
6						

WHATS SHEET

No		Gold	Red	Blue	Black	White
7						
8						
9						
10						
11						
12						

Once you have completed your draft list of Whats, pause and look them over again. This time you need to seek God again and ask Him – which of these are of you Lord and which ones might be coming just from me?

Here you are seeking Him intently and listening for His still small voice. If you then think some might not be specifically God-given just put a single line through that What but do not erase or obliterate it.

Once you have a list, even if each is not that clear or detailed, it's time to try to provide more detail and focus by conducting these three reviews.

1 – THE WHO REVIEW

Review your list line by line, this time consider each specifically, whether there is a particular target group you would like to work with. The list below might help. If you do identify a specific group then update the What to include the group.

- Gender
- Children: What age from and to?
- Young people: What age from and to?
- Adults: What age from and to?
- Abilities/Disabilities: If so, which?
- Medical conditions: If so, which?
- Background: unemployed, self-employed, management, leaders, business owners, prisoners, other.
- Secular/Christian/Other Faith?
- Ethnic group: If so, which?
- Other groups: If so, which?

2 – THE NEEDS REVIEW

Each review is to help you become clearer in what God has put on your heart, just as a photographer focuses the lens in or out to get a clearer picture. This review can help you be clearer on how those you want to work with in your What can benefit. Look at the list of needs below and try to identify what the needs are which you really want to meet in your Whats.

- Physical
- Emotional
- Relational
- Educational
- Vocational
- Sexual
- Spiritual

A person I was working with in going through this programme, said that all they could initially identify as a What was that "I know I want to work with young people." That gave us a place to start, although it needed more definition. By using The Who Review the person said that there were really two different age groups: firstly, the 0–3s, and secondly the mid to late teens. There was a willingness to work with males or females and did not mind if they were Christians, but also wanted to reach non-Christians as well. Clarification was achieved using The Who Review.

Applying The Needs Review identified that this person wanted to meet the physical and emotional needs of the 0–3s and the emotional and spiritual needs of the mid to late teens groups. This was useful as when applying this review that person realised that this What would require very different action for each of these two groups. Therefore, they realised that they needed to split this into two separate Whats. This, although now seemingly obvious, was very useful as it was now becoming much clearer for them. They then prioritised the work with the teens over the 0–3s because it was at the gold centre of their target. They did not want to lose their vision for the 0–3s but now realised that this would be a longer-term project which they could not start until they had established the work with the teens.

ACTION - Please now review your Whats List and include the needs you would like to help meet in the target group.

3 – THE PRIORITY REVIEW

This review is to help you understand which of your Whats are more important than the others. This is so that you can allocate your 3 Ts wisely. On the right of your Whats Sheet are columns, gold, red etc. These are based on the colours of the archery target, with gold at the centre working outwards.

Review each What and put a tick in the colour column which you believe is the right one. Ask God to help you here. You really need to be clear and settled on this, no matter how hard it is. You CANNOT have more than one number one priority. If you have, for example, two that you feel are both gold priorities, then choose 'Gold No. 1' and 'Gold No. 2'.

I worked with someone who had two gold centre Whats which they said they could not prioritise over the other. So, I asked them to write each What on separate pieces of paper. I then said that I want you to hold onto the one which is most important to you and give me the other. The next few moments were spent watching that person anguish over the decision and after some time they handed me one and kept the other. When I got home that night, I received a phone call from that person to say that they had made the right decision. A liberating moment for them.

Giving a priority doesn't mean that you will never action the lesser priority Whats; it just means that you know which are more important. This is a really important review and can really help to remove the last bits of fog from your mind and bring the clarity you need. If you are finding it hard to differentiate between some Whats, ask the question **"If I can only achieve one of these Whats in the remainder of my life, which one would it be?"**

MOVING ON

So, by now you will hopefully have a prioritised list of Whats even if possibly quite a way from being fully defined, which you will have reviewed to identify any specific target groups you would like to work with and which needs you would like to meet for each individual What. You will also hopefully by now have also identified:

- Your spiritual gifts from the 5-fold ministry areas;

- Your Personality of structured/unstructured/task/people preference; and

- Positive and negative experiences in life to date which help frame your view of life.

Before we go on to look at how all this might fit together and the part each of these plays let's keep the end of this programme in mind. The desired end result is that you will have:

- A list of Whats which are clear and unambiguous, and

- Which show you what to do, who you want to do it with, along with a plan of action that will allow you to see the initial steps you will take, steps which are in line with your spiritual gifts and natural strengths and geared around your unique personality, driven by God-given motivation.

There, nothing to it really is there? But the desired end result is to at least get to Step 3 of that earlier framework (See page 12). Step 1 was to Dream; Step 2 was to Dare and Step 3 to Create.

If you do not break down your Whats to the point where you know the first steps to take you can get stuck in Steps 1 and 2. Wouldn't that be a tragedy? That is why you need not just to know your identity in God, but to stand on it and push on to create.

You will face some Giants along the way. Even now, thoughts like, "This is all too difficult and complicated," or "I haven't got the time for this. I still can't see this clearly" and "I'll put this off until later on" may be coming to mind.

You will need to use your mind and your will to overcome these and your other Giants and prioritise the use of your 3 Ts to make your dreams in God come true. The alternative is to carry on doing what you have always been doing and miss out on the fulfilment you know you want to get from living the rest of your life.

Now might be a good time to go back to the declaration you read aloud and signed earlier and read it aloud all over again (See page 21) and ensure you are really committed to your Destiny. So, turning your Whats into reality will require you to take action but identifying what action to take is not always so easy for some people. It comes more easily to some than others, but it is vital even if you don't find it easy.

So, here is a framework for action planning which can help you. It is a commonly used one and it is known as SMART.

S – SPECIFIC
Any action you take needs to be clear and unambiguous otherwise you don't know where to start and everything seems a fog. Be specific. Action needs to be broken down to the point where there is nothing to stop you from taking the first step, even if it is towards a seemingly huge vision or dream. The smallest step you do take is better than the largest one you don't take.

M – MEASURABLE
Action needs to be clear enough in definition so that you will know when you have taken it. For example, your first step might be to research where in the area other things similar to your What are being done. This you will know will be completed when you have finished carrying out the research you identified. Your progress is therefore measurable.

A – ACHIEVEABLE
In Christian terms we know we need to depend on God and not do things in our own strength. Yet when God gives us an understanding of His plan and we know it is from Him there is action we need to take. Achievable here means that in relation to God's plan there is nothing now preventing you from taking that step, other than your own will. Break the action down so that the first step is sufficiently small enough for you to take.

R – RELEVANT
It needs to be relevant to your specific What. If the action doesn't relate to your What it is off-target. Adjust it so that it will relate to and progress your What.

T – TIMELY
Having worked out the SMAR for your action now set yourself a clear target date by which you will complete it. Be realistic with yourself in setting this date. It should only be just far enough ahead to allow you to complete it. Don't let the Giant of procrastination win here. Don't let the Giant of distraction come in and stop you keeping to your plan. If needs be make yourself accountable to someone else for achieving your action plan. After all, it is your plan to progress your God-given dreams and potential.

ACTION – Bringing it all together. This might seem straightforward to you, or you may be thinking, I don't like planning; I just like to get on and do things. Whichever way, you need to keep the end in mind which is to get to Step Three and start creating. Let's look at how this all fits together, based on a real-life example I have experience with. I've called the person this is based on 'Elliott' to preserve their anonymity.

Do you see the gateway is now more open than you might have first thought, but you still have to walk through it? Don't stand on the outside of your Destiny just looking in. Walk through into all that God has for you and start living as you have always wanted to. Jesus came to give us life and life abundant (John 10:10). Abundant means just that, more than enough for you personally so that you can be a blessing to others.

TARGETS CASE STUDY – ELLIOT

Elliott's 5-fold ministry result showed Pastor as a top spiritual gifting but also Teacher. A key experience in his life was feeling quite lonely as a child even though he had brothers and sisters, however they were either much older or younger. Elliott also came to know great joy when some of that loneliness lifted on him becoming a Christian.

He is also structured and task-focused and borders on being people-focused.

ELLIOTT'S WHAT

Elliott struggled to be clear with a What. The starting place we got to for their key What was "Getting alongside the lonely."

I asked Elliott, "How would you actually do this", but despite being an educated, articulate person, he did not know this clearly at all. This was a source of frustration to him. So we applied the process to this What. We had this starting place and knew that this was something that was really on his heart to do, and believed was God-given.

YOUR WHAT

Let's use this process and Elliott's experience together so that we go through it in tandem with one of your Whats. We still may not come up with a perfect answer, but the chances are that it will be better than where you are with your What at the moment. It might be good to take one of your more important Whats and if one is still a bit vague or nebulous use that one and write it just as it is in the space below.

My What is:

....
....
....
....
....
....
....
....
....
....
....
....
....

ELLIOTT'S WHO REVIEW

Elliott's Who Review brought out that he wanted to work with men, Christians but not exclusively so. This could include young adults but these would predominantly be older adults. So, this added an extra amount of focus which we did not have before.

YOUR WHO REVIEW

(See page 38 for the categories)

Write the result of your own Who Review of the What you wish to work with:

....
....
....
....
....
....
....

ELLIOTT'S NEEDS REVIEW

Elliott, as said earlier, struggled to clearly define this What, but by applying this step we identified that in relation to the target group Elliott wanted to meet primarily the emotional but also the spiritual needs of the preferred target group, even though he still had no real focus on how. I can tell you that Elliott did know, but just struggled to put it into words clearly and had been this way for many years. I can tell you that you do know, and you can, with perseverance, come out with a clearer focus than you have had before. The Needs Review helped Elliott as the picture was building to indicate a willingness to work with adult men, Christians but not exclusively, for whom he wanted to meet emotional needs primarily, but also spiritual needs.

YOUR NEEDS REVIEW

Write your Needs Review for your own What in the space below:

....
....
....
....
....
....
....

ELLIOTT'S EXPERIENCES

We had a broad outline of Elliott's What which was "Getting alongside the lonely" and the lonely for him meant male, mainly Christian, mainly adult, but no other real detail. He had that experience of being lonely or at least feeling lonely as a child, but which lifted when he became a Christian. But I wanted to probe this What more, so we broke it down into two parts:

1. The lonely; and
2. Getting alongside.

I asked Elliott what 'lonely' meant. He replied that it was someone who spent a lot of time alone but wanted to be with other people. He linked it back to the sense of isolation he felt as a child. So, there was a direct link with one of his personal, even if negative, life experiences. I believe the linkage between a What and a key life experience can be another possible signpost that God has been shaping you for this purpose. However, I don't believe the absence of such a link restricts it from being part of God's plan. Rather, I would see it as a question mark which is worth looking at more fully but keeping an open mind towards.

Elliott had paused after this but clearly had something else in mind, so I asked, "What else does lonely mean to you other than isolated?" He replied, "It is also feeling rejected." This was also another aspect of what he felt when spending time alone as a child. He wanted to play with older siblings, but they were so much older that they had friends and interests of their own.

Elliott realised it was not their fault but still had a sense of rejection which added to the sense of isolation. So 'the lonely' for Elliott meant those men feeling isolated through having to spend long periods alone but also included those who felt a sense of rejection. We then looked at the second part which was 'getting alongside,' as Elliott was still far from clear on how to achieve this What. Whatever this meant, we now knew it included meeting primarily the emotional but also, if possible, the spiritual needs of his preferred target group.

With this in mind I asked Elliott what 'getting alongside' meant in relation to these emotional and spiritual needs. Again, the answer was a shrug of the shoulders and a frustrated look on his face followed by "I don't really know." I then said, "Close your eyes and begin to visualise that you have "come alongside" someone and it is 100% successful. Describe to me what you are actually doing." Elliott did that and in just a few moments said: "I am listening to them. That is so important, giving someone who is feeling lonely and rejected time to talk, and givin them my full attention by just being there to listen."

I said "What else are you doing?" He replied "I am also, as well as allowing them time to talk, telling them of my similar experiences but I am telling them they can come through this to live a life with joy." So getting alongside had gone from being an unknown quantity to now listening, really listening, and being able to share similar experiences with the person and also encouragement that the person can come through this time. We also discovered that getting alongside was mainly, but not exclusively, in a one-to-one situation.

Again, I asked, "What are you doing?" and he replied "I am telling the person what God says about them. How He loves them and is always with them. I want them to know God, as I came to know Him, and to have the joy from that relationship which overcomes the loneliness, and I am praying with them." So now getting alongside meant, in relation to the target group:

- One-to-one situations mainly;
- Really listening and giving real space to talk;
- Sharing similar experiences;
- Explaining God's view of that person from the Bible;
- Encouragement that the loneliness/rejection can be overcome; and
- Praying with that person.

So, we were making some real progress and Elliott's fog, and sense of frustration were beginning to lift a bit and he was beginning to get a little excited that a dream was starting to come to life. We then reflected back to his spiritual gifts which were Pastoral and Teaching and there seemed to be a good fit here. Through this What, Elliot was able to show care and support people and so could now have some increased confidence that he was on target.

YOUR EXPERIENCES

Write down if there is a link between any of your experiences and your own What. Also, any clarification the experiences bring to the What.

……………………………………………………………………………………………………
……………………………………………………………………………………………………
……………………………………………………………………………………………………
……………………………………………………………………………………………………
……………………………………………………………………………………………………
……………………………………………………………………………………………………
……………………………………………………………………………………………………
……………………………………………………………………………………………………
……………………………………………………………………………………………………
……………………………………………………………………………………………………
……………………………………………………………………………………………………
……………………………………………………………………………………………………
……………………………………………………………………………………………………
……………………………………………………………………………………………………
……………………………………………………………………………………………………
……………………………………………………………………………………………………
……………………………………………………………………………………………………
……………………………………………………………………………………………………
……………………………………………………………………………………………………
……………………………………………………………………………………………………
……………………………………………………………………………………………………
……………………………………………………………………………………………………

Break your What down into component parts, then visualise yourself carrying out each part in a way that is 100% successful. Write down in the space below what you are doing and the situation / environment etc. Write down everything you are doing which is contributing to that success and which gives you information about your What. Be prepared to think deeply. Don't accept second best from yourself here; push on. Visualise this several times until you are happy you have captured all the information you need for clarification. Use deep, prayerful thinking. Don't accept superficiality.

………………………………………………………………………………………………………
………………………………………………………………………………………………………
………………………………………………………………………………………………………
………………………………………………………………………………………………………
………………………………………………………………………………………………………
………………………………………………………………………………………………………
………………………………………………………………………………………………………
………………………………………………………………………………………………………
………………………………………………………………………………………………………
………………………………………………………………………………………………………
………………………………………………………………………………………………………
………………………………………………………………………………………………………
………………………………………………………………………………………………………
………………………………………………………………………………………………………
………………………………………………………………………………………………………
………………………………………………………………………………………………………
………………………………………………………………………………………………………
………………………………………………………………………………………………………

ELLIOTT'S PERSONALITY

Having reached this stage, we were still short of some specific detail we needed. We had made good progress but still had a little way to go. What we didn't know was how the "getting alongside" would start, and where it would end. Personality would play a part here.

Elliott visualised a one-to-one meeting doing the things identified earlier. But how did he and the person get to be in the one to one and at what point would Elliott's getting alongside end. If you think about the one to one it could be in many different situations: out on the street, at his house, the other person's house, at a hostel, church etc. And how did he meet the other person? Did they find the person or did the person come to them?

I asked Elliott how the successful one to one, as visualised, came about. Did he see someone in the High Street sitting on a seat looking lonely, who he then initiated a conversation with? I suspected I knew the answer already. The response was noticeably instant. "No, I wouldn't just go out and speak to people on the street, that's just not me, I wouldn't like that." I asked, "So how would this one to one come about." He preferred to meet with someone who knew what they would be meeting for and also preferably that the person would know in advance that the meeting would include a time to talk and be listened to with some sharing of experience, prayer and scriptural advice. Elliott is structured and benefits from a structured environment so this would be a good way to work.

I then asked him "At what point would you consider you had fully succeeded in achieving your What with that person and the coming alongside would conclude?" The answer was "I am not sure." I said "You could meet with this person for months, even years, or for a few minutes. You could become a mentor to them, possibly for the future."

Elliott said "No. I don't want to mentor or anything like that. I don't want long-term. So, I asked "At what point would your involvement end in a way that keeps you happy? At what point would you feel you had succeeded in meeting the emotional and spiritual needs you want to meet?" Elliott replied: "I suppose I want to help them achieve a level of initial emotional stability and to have a better understanding of God's love for them, plus some hope and encouragement that they can get through the loneliness or rejection. Then I would like someone else who can develop them further, to take them on from me."

The answers to these questions are really important as we need to know where our giftings and abilities start and just as importantly end. We need to know how we can work in line with our personality, which is unique.

Elliott's support was on the shorter side at the point of "initial emotional stability."

He has a strong sense of responsibility and hates to let anyone down, so knowing where his gifts and talents end is important. Elliott would feel real responsibility for the time with the other person. Unless he was clear on the point at which his part ended there could well be a real sense of feeling he had let the other person down. That potentially would adversely affect Elliott, and lead him to stay in the situation beyond the point of still feeling happy.

Elliott now knows that point, and needs to action this What in a way that will avoid the potential difficulties but maintain maximum success by having someone to hand that person over to. Elliott is also a structured person in personality terms but is only just more task than people focused. Being structured, he likes things to be clearly defined and likes relationships to be consistent.

These personality preferences influence the inception of the one-to-one meetings for him, with a preference to meeting people in clearly defined situations. So, it is no surprise that Elliott would prefer the other person to know what they were going to meet for, and Elliott indicated that having someone come to them as a referral would be much better with the other person also knowing in advance when his involvement would cease.

Working in line with our spiritual gifts, natural abilities, personality, and experiences makes sense. It works best for us. So, we each need, and you need, to action plan your own What in a way which is as much in line with the way God made you as possible. Plan and build for success by aligning your strengths, not your weaknesses.

YOUR PERSONALITY

Now review your What again and in the space below write down how you think these aspects might shape your What. Include how it would best reflect your personality. Think hard and deeply – it will save you a lot of time and frustration later.

....
....
....
....
....
....
....
....
....
....
....
....
....
....
....
....
....

The John West Test

At the beginning of writing your Whats I encouraged you to write everything down and not filter anything out. This was to ensure that you did not miss anything which is of real importance. You should by now have also prioritised your list of Whats via the archery target colours of **Gold, Red, Blue, Black and White.**

Each of us has the 3 Ts of Time, Talent, and Treasure but not the same combination of each. There was an advert on TV years ago which said, "It is the fish that John West rejects which makes John West the best." There is a similarity with us. We just cannot do everything as we don't have the 3 Ts to do so. If we devote our resources to things which are of lesser importance to us and to God, rather than those most important we might just be hitting the target, but we won't be hitting our gold centre.

So now is a good time to review your Whats again and to ask God to let you know any which are not really in His plan for you. Let God know you want His will only to be done in your life. Listen deeply for the still small voice and delete any which you believe should no longer be on the list. This leaves more 3 Ts for the others.

ELLIOTT'S SMART TEST

We are almost there now. We have covered quite a bit of ground in this Targets Section, but we need to focus on the end result and to get specific about the action necessary to take first steps. So, let's go back to Elliott's What and apply the SMART framework to it.

Elliott's What – Getting alongside the lonely.

We know that he prefers one-to-one situations, a more structured meeting process and a clearly defined beginning and end. However, he was also prepared to meet people in church who he would actually approach if they were on their own. So, this gives him some greater clarity, but first steps are still needed. He needs a way of getting to meet with those people. So how can this come about? It won't happen with things as they are now.

Without an action plan you won't turn your dreams into reality, You NEED to make a start if you are genuine in your aspirations. So, applying the SMART framework is vital. Please do not move ahead without doing so. Not having a SMART action plan will allow the Giants of procrastination and distraction to attack you mercilessly.

SPECIFIC – What specific action could Elliott take? A suggestion appears next, and you can think of others. Elliott should speak to the church leader about his What and ask to be able to have lonely people referred by others, with there being someone else to whom he can pass that person over to in time. That is specific action.

MEASURABLE – It is measurable in that it is easy to know when it has been done by having that conversation with one of the leaders.

ACHIEVABLE – It is a short piece of action. Booking an appointment to see the church leader is easily achievable by Elliott. As a very first step. This is in his power to do and so there is nothing to stop him from making that appointment other than his will. Focus on breaking the action for each of your Whats down to the point of there being nothing to stop you.

RELEVANT – Yes, it is directly related to achieving the What, so definitely relevant.

TIMELY – Elliott needs to set a short period in which to achieve this. A week should be enough. Do set a definite time period and ensure it is as short as necessary to allow achievement through taking positive action. This will overcome the Giant of procrastination.

You might have a much larger What such as wanting to feed the homeless, but you have to start somewhere. Breaking the action down into small pieces is vital and for the first step break it down to the point where there is nothing preventing you at all (other than your own will) from taking that step.

YOUR SMART TEST

YOUR OWN ACTION PLAN – In the space below write out a SMART action plan for one of your Whats. Specific, Measurable, Achieveable, Relevant and Timely.

S

M

A

R

T

PROPHETIC WORDS

One area I haven't touched on yet is Prophetic Words you may have been given in your life to date. This is a difficult area due to how accurate or inaccurate the word(s) spoken to you might be. I would suggest that such words given to you by others should NOT be what leads you to a What but rather may give indication that a What you have already identified in your time with God, is for you. All prophetic words should be weighed prayerfully and carefully before taking note of, accepting or actioning.

In summary you have covered and should now be able to understand:

- You are an Arrow in God's hand;
- The key Whats you believe are in God's plan for your life;
- How your spiritual gifts can influence you. Your 5-fold ministry results can also give you additional insight into how God has wired you to be;
- How your natural abilities can influence you;
- How your personality can influence you;
- How your positive and negative life experiences can influence you; and
- How you can break necessary action down to a point where you can take the first step.

When I got to this point, I realised that I had reached a real landmark and important point. This point was that I had run out of excuses for now not taking action. I knew what to do and what my first step was to be. I had no excuses left. If my dreams were to be realised, and I was not going to live a life of regrets, I had to take responsibility for my dreams and take the first steps to create. You need to do the same.

Life Mission

I outlined earlier my Life Mission. To get to that point I looked over my list of Whats and carefully reviewed them to see if there might be something linking them together. If there is a linkage this might just be your Life Mission. Several times over several different days I looked at my list and couldn't see any link at all. But then surprisingly one day I did perceive a link.

All of my Whats had an element of wanting to see people develop fully into what God has for them. If you do get to this point, just write down what you perceive a link might be even if you just have the gist of it. Then, once that is done try to get this reduced down to one or two sentences by further reviewing and deleting every word that is just padding or duplication. There might not be a link between your Whats so don't get hung up on this. However, if there is do note it down.

Once I had my Life Mission down to 23 words, I happened to be reading my Bible one day when I read Ephesians 1:1. This says (NIV) – "Paul, an apostle of Christ Jesus by the will of God" …. Now I had read these mere eleven words many times before but now it really meant something beautiful and valuable to me. I had usually read it as a basic introduction from Paul to the Ephesian Church but having just gone through my Life Mission process I began to see it very differently. How and why was I seeing it differently?

Because in eleven words St Paul identified himself by name, he said what he was (an Apostle), who's he was (of Jesus Christ) and that he was in the will of God.

I could not help but stop and reread this many times. I became aware that this was Paul's Life Mission there in eleven words. I was acutely aware of what Paul had to have stripped out of his life to get down to this in so few words.

Can you say what you are, who's you are and declare that the life you are living is in the will of God? Paul had taken direct responsibility for the life and calling God had given him. Are you prepared to do the same? God bless you in your Godly dreams and aspirations.

EAGLES

The next section will look at how to develop good attitudes and habits which will allow you to really get the best out of yourself and will definitely be of help to you if you want to move to Steps 4 and 5 of the framework, which are Step 4, to Grow and Step 5, to Expand.

Thank you for progressing this far with GATEway to Destiny and for reviewing your life and what you are doing with it. I have already mentioned about our journey from Convert to Disciple and will feature more about this now as I see discipleship as the foundation for excelling in God. This journey will require of you ever greater degrees of surrender to God. This surrender needs to be perceived by us as something of value, something beneficial. But how is surrender beneficial to us? Because we must decrease that He might increase (John 3:30). The more we surrender to God the more His Kingdom grows. Andrew Murray has much to say about this in his book *Absolute Surrender*. The Bible also teaches us clearly on this and I have listed some of the key scriptures here.

Eagles are one of the most impressive and formidable of birds on this earth. They have legendary eyesight and are known to be able to soar higher than most other birds. When soaring on thermals with wings fully extended, they are magnificent, majestic birds with brilliant eyesight to focus on prey from great distance.

So, by studying Eagles and applying some of the principles to our own life we might well be able to learn things of help to us. It is an interesting thought that Giants are irrelevant to Eagles, as Eagles inhabit the heights, not the ground. Eagles are mentioned many times in the Bible and possibly the most well used verse is in Isaiah 40:31 "Those who hope in the Lord will renew their strength; they will soar on wings like eagles…"

Hope in God will help us soar like an Eagle. When seeking to fulfil God's plan and purpose for our life we need to "hope in the Lord" if we really want to do the best we can. We are designed to soar, not caw with crows but to push on to reach our full potential. Not to settle for second-best or to sell our potential short.

Galatians 2:20 (ESV) – "I have been crucified with Christ. It is no longer I who live, but Christ who lives in me. And the life I now live in the flesh I live by faith in the Son of God, who loved me and gave himself for me."

Jeremiah 10:23 (NIV) – "Lord I know that people's lives are not their own; it is not for them to direct their steps."

Romans 12:1 (NKJV) – "I beseech you therefore, brethren by the mercies of God, that you present your bodies as a living sacrifice, holy, acceptable to God, which is your reasonable service."

Luke 9:23-24 (ESV) – "And he said to all, 'If anyone would come after me, let him deny himself and take up his cross daily and follow me. For whoever would save his life will lose it, but whoever loses his life for my sake will save it'."

Philippians 1:21(ESV) – "For to me, to live is Christ and to die is gain." Surrendering to God can be hard but it is also joy. Do you remember how in the garden the night before His death Jesus agonised over what pain and suffering, He was to go through. The whipping, the torment, the nails, and the pain. Luke 22:43-44. Yet Jesus did it. He at the age of 33 gave up His life for us. Absolute surrender, absolute obedience, and the result; absolute victory for the Kingdom of God.

Our surrender needs to be seen by us in the light of His surrender. As Andrew Murray says, "Christ will come into you with the power of His death and the power of His life: and then the Holy Spirit will bring the whole Christ – Christ crucified and risen and living in glory – into your heart."

Our Whats have to be His Whats so we live the life God has for us however long or short that life may be. None of us are guaranteed tomorrow – life really is a privilege and not a right. Jesus did not have a long life. Our Life Mission has to be His Life Mission. We have to be His disciples and take up our cross daily. This entails leaving aside what we want to do for what He wants us to do.

In Matthew 28:16-20 (NASV) it says "But the eleven disciples proceeded to Galilee, to the mountain which Jesus had designated to them. And when they saw Him, they worshipped Him, but some were doubtful. And Jesus came up to them saying 'All authority in heaven and on earth has been given to me. Go, therefore and make disciples of all nations, baptising them in the name of the father and the Son and the Holy Spirit, teaching them to follow all that I have commanded you; and behold, I am with you always, to the end of the age'."

What strikes me about this Great Commission is the sheer importance of it to Jesus. Why do I say that? Because He came back from the dead to bring His disciples this message and what a message. He clearly and simply told them what He wanted them to do with the remainder of their collective lives. He also told them of the authority He had been given and in which they were to Go.

Read these verses again. How much authority has Jesus been given? The answer is ALL. Not just a bit but ALL. So, if Jesus has ALL the authority how much can the enemy have? The answer is only that which we give him. That which he can deceive us out of as he has NO authority of his own. And what assurance did Jesus give them? That He would be with them always and to the end of the age. Wonderful. When our Whats are His Whats we can be confident of Jesus being with us always.

When Jesus was in His ministry prior to His death the Pharisees tried to test Him by asking "Teacher, what is the most important commandment in the law? Jesus answered "Love the Lord your God with all your heart, soul, and mind. This is the first and most important commandment. The second most important commandment is like this one. And it is to love others as much as you love yourself. All the law of Moses and the Books of the Prophets are based on these two commandments." Matthew 22:36-40 (CEV).

A friend of mine wisely said "You will never achieve the Great Commission without first living the Great Commandment". To go deeper with Surrender to God we each need to go deeper in our love for Him. The more love for Him the more we willingly surrender. That is me decreasing that He might increase lived out. We can never or should ever get so wrapped up in our Whats that we neglect our relationship with Him. If they are truly His Whats we need to put Him first and keep Him first. This is keeping the first things first. "Seek ye first the Kingdom of God and His righteousness and all these things shall be added unto you." Matthew 6:33 (KJV).

Within my time as a Leadership and Management Trainer I have read much on motivation. Generally, there are two main types of it: extrinsic and intrinsic. Extrinsic is motivation that comes to a person from an external source. For instance, offering someone a cash bonus for doing a particularly good job. If the person offered, accepts, and does better work than he or she would have done without the bonus then the motivation from outside has worked. This is extrinsic as it came for outside of the individual.

The other type is intrinsic. This comes from inside the person his or herself. For instance, if a person has values which dictate to him or her that they will do the best job they can even if there is no supervisor watching over them then this is intrinsic motivation. It comes from within that person and no external source is needed.

I suggest to you that it is the love we have for God that generates and sustains our intrinsic motivation. It is the source of it. We aren't dependent on an outside source to press on, we rely on our Love for God. Longer term we will need our Intrinsic motivation to be strong and ongoing to be able to push through our Giants to be all that we can be in God. Perhaps now is a good time to reflect again on how passionate we still are for God. If you sense some depletion in your passion, go back to Him and allow the flames to be fanned again. We are all human and we leak. But God is faithful to refill and refuel us if we ask Him and allow Him. This isn't weakness it is strength.

God takes our love for Him seriously. Just to confirm this look at Revelation 2:4. The Church in Ephesus is commended by God for many good things in its favour. Then in verse 4 it says (NIV) "Yet I hold this against you. You have forsaken the love you had at first. Consider how far you have fallen! Repent and do the things you did at first". We each need to keep the first things first in our life.

This brings me on to another point. We aren't good at everything are we? This means that for a growing ministry we need people with additional skills to complement the areas we aren't strong in. Perhaps administration, finance or communications skills might be needed. We need help from others. Be open and transparent about this.

We also need a continual high level of integrity every day. Finance is an example. A ministry needs to be open and honest and take great care over financial matters. High standards of morality are also important. You have no doubt heard of Christian men and women in high profile ministries who have had to resign due to having an extra-marital affair. This destroys both personal and ministry reputations as well as hurts many people.

So how do we guard against this happening? By having people work with us and to whom we give our explicit expressed permission to speak into EVERY area of our life including finance, relationships, and behaviour. Even if we do not want to be accountable to others we need to be so. It is in the best interests of ourselves and the growing ministry we are part of. To not do so risks being able to hide things from other people and this invariably leads to downfall and all the pain that comes with it.

So, a few points for you on the theme of Eagles.

1. Who are you flying with?

Are you associating with people who will help you become who God wants you to be. Make a list of those Christians you spend most time with and be honest with yourself. Are they helping you in growing as a Christian? If 'Yes', fine but if not, who can you associate with who can help you and who perhaps in turn you could help.

Do you meet with anyone who you can talk to about your Godly dreams and aspirations? Find someone who can help with your accountability for your life and aspirations.

....
....
....
....
....

2. Are all my characteristics Eagle-like or are some from other birds?

As said throughout this workbook character is important to us as Christians. Make an honest assessment of your character but remember, "There is no condemnation for those who are in Christ Jesus" (Romans 8:1) this is an assessment rooted in knowing God's love for and delight in us – it is to help us not condemn us.

Ask God to help you in any areas of weakness and go to a friend you can trust and ask to speak to them about anything you are struggling with or have doubts about. Look at the Fruit of the Spirit in Galatians 5:22 – Love, joy, peace, patience, kindness, goodness, faithfulness, gentleness, and self-control. Ask God to help you in each of these areas specifically.

....
....
....
....
....
....
....
....

3. Do I soar above problems or am I limited by them?

How do you react when things don't go your way? Can you keep your own emotions in check and understand that if the problem comes through another person that God loves that person just as much as He loves you and that you are speaking to a brother or sister? Don't be surprised when situations like this come your way as the best way you can learn to rise like an Eagle above the storm is to meet and deal with storms. Can you think of times when you were passive rather than active in your growth as a Christian and times when you gave up when you should not have done so? Resolve now to be an overcomer. Get up, dust yourself off and go again.

....
....
....
....
....
....
....

4. Do I have an Eagle diet?

What are you feeding yourself on spiritually? To be a top athlete you have to have the right diet. It's the same spiritually so are you feeding on the Word of God and more than just feeding do as the Bible says which is to meditate on the Word day and night. To meditate means to focus your mind and in particular you need to not just read the Bible but to apply it to every aspect of your life. James 1:22 advises us not to be just hearers of the Word but doers.

Write out a diet list – what you will feed on now and what you will remove from your current spiritual diet.

....
....
....
....
....
....
....
....

Linked to this is your actual food diet. Are you looking after the body you have? Do you feed it properly with a sensible amount of good food to keep yourself healthy enough to have the energy and longevity to outwork your Whats well. This is something I have struggled with in the past and in part still do now but is something I am actively working on now.

....
....
....
....
....
....
....
....
....

5. How do I deal with serpents?

Snakes are enemies of Eagles and will try to kill their young, but Eagles will tear the heads off snakes if they catch them. They do not tolerate snakes.

Are you aware of how the enemy tries to intimidate or defeat you? Learn to understand your areas of greatest temptation and vulnerability and devise a strategy or strategies to overcome these areas. For example, if alcohol causes you to behave badly what will you do to prevent that from happening. You need a strategy which works for you. Be honest, be real and do not be passive, rise, act, and tear the head off what is coming against you. Do not tolerate things you know you should not be tolerating.

....
....
....
....
....
....
....
....

6. How do I deal with weariness?

Tiredness is something we all suffer from to varying degrees or in specific circumstances. Are you getting the right amount of rest and relaxation and above all time alone with God. What unproductive things do you need to remove from your life in order to spend time with God? Time management is vital. It's the one of our 3 Ts we do not get back. Once time is gone it is gone. Ask Him to help you review your time and activities to allow you to become an Eagle. You will need to root out unproductive activities from your schedule if you want to hit the gold centre of your target. Weariness is not an excuse for poor standards of conduct or behaviour. Do not let your Giants stop you from starting, slow you down or lead you on to non-productive paths. Consider whether you are looking after the body you have been given. Are you getting enough quality sleep to keep up with what you need to do at a high level?

....
....
....
....
....

7. How do I stay fit to soar?

An Eagle will set aside time for checking its own feathers to make sure they are in good condition and even pluck out some that are not so that it can soar as it needs to. Keep a focus on your own personal growth and development and have regular honest reviews of your Christian journey and effectiveness. Look for and pluck out anything that is not of God, and which might hinder you. Are you getting the right amount of exercise to keep your body in good shape to help ward off avoidable illnesses and injuries.

....
....
....
....
....

8. Am I really soaring or just flying high?

Be honest with yourself and don't settle for mediocrity. Allow God to show you what He has for you and partner with Him in excellence. Don't expect perfection in yourself as you will never find it and be constantly frustrated but do look to be excellent in God's work.

....
....
....
....
....

9. How am I with commitment to my potential?

Am I focused on growing day by day? Do I learn from experiences or keep on making the same mistakes? At the end of each day stop and think. Ask yourself, 'What went well AND why?" Ask yourself, "What didn't go so well AND again why?" It doesn't have to take long. You can go through this process quickly with just a little practice and it will help you to discover and repeat the things making your day go well and start to eliminate those things that do not.

……………………………………………………………………………………………………
……………………………………………………………………………………………………
……………………………………………………………………………………………………
……………………………………………………………………………………………………
……………………………………………………………………………………………………
……………………………………………………………………………………………………
……………………………………………………………………………………………………
……………………………………………………………………………………………………

It is my view that it is your spiritual giftings and natural talents which determine how successful you can become in your God-given dreams and aspirations. However, it is the combination of these with your character that will determine the actual level of success you have and how long that success will last.

GATEway TO DESTINY

Eagles who inspire me

Before ending this Section I would like to mention a few Eagles who inspire me, who are flying high and will only fly higher in their God-given callings.

Barrie Townsend from Exmouth, England. Barrie is my long-time colleague and co-founder of Crosslink Transformation Network (CTN). Barrie is Mr. Eagle to me. A former senior manager / director in the Motor Trade with a huge heart for people and seeing them grow as people as well as employees. I pay great tribute to him as he still has a strong desire to see people become proficient leaders as he recognises the huge importance of good leadership with focus on looking after and developing people. In particular, I thank him for his willing input into this Eagles section. His willingness to study the Bible is immense and as strong as ever.

Chris and Kerry Cole based in Plymouth, England. Chris is the Chairman of Cornerstone Vision Ltd a media company, which started the international radio ministry, Cross Rhythms. He is also a church leader and trustee of GOD TV and the Christian Broadcasting Council. Kerry is an established author of a number of books including The Purple Veil, Exit Darcus and Gotta Die to Live. They have been married since 1982 and have three daughters and four grandchildren. *(chrisandkerrycole.com)*

Peter Lawry, from New Zealand - international speaker, SME business strategist and author of When Jesus Calls: Transforming businesses into expressions of God's Kingdom. Having discovered the power and joy of surrendering his business entirely to God as his CEO, Peter now mentors others to do the same. His business advisory company is Business As Mission Limited, New Zealand.
(business-as-mission.com)

Tim Moyler, who is part of Agape UK and has developed the 'Living and Telling' course to help Christians grow in confidence in sharing their faith. This is now spreading rapidly around the UK and is now going international helping countless people share Jesus with others. Youth Course, 'Live it, Tell it'.
(livingandtelling.org.uk)

Paul Bulkeley, architect at Snug Architects and founder of bizMIN who has created a course with a mission to call and equip a new generation of Christian entrepreneurs to do business as ministry. *(bizmin.org)*

Jim Grimmer from Aberdeen who set up and runs P3 Business Care. P3 is a social enterprise operating across the UK and now internationally to help businesses manage the problems their employees have so they don't impact one's business. Jim has a heart to help people within the workplace setting to help the wellbeing of staff and through that the business.
(p3businesscare.com)

Alistair Gibson, published author and founder of Countdown Creative Ltd, a content creation company in Exeter. Alistair models servant heartedness and helps his clients develop a greater online presence via SEO articles, diverse blog sites and social media platforms.
(www.countdowncreative.co.uk)

All of the these have a vison for their unique life and are faithfully outworking what they believe God has called them to do. You can do the same in whatever God is calling you to do no matter how large or small.

Embrace your destiny

Remember who you are, what you are and who's you are. Don't let your Giants deceive you. Remember some additional Eagle thoughts and attitudes below.

- God loves me like no other can;
- He has a plan and purpose for my life;
- He has created me as a weapon in His hand;
- We are destined to Soar with Eagles;
- I make my greatest impact with my spiritual gifting and natural abilities;
- I have been created with mind, emotions and will;
- Eagles make time to get cleaned up;
- Eagles realise they aren't born into a life of ease but a life of discipline;
- I can use my mind to listen to God's Word or the world's word;
- I can use my mind to control my emotions;
- I can use Godly emotions to influence my mind positively;
- The choices I make can be positive ones or passive ones but either way it is my decision;
- It is my sensitivity to God and my obedience to Him which are the flights of my arrow;
- I have been given Time, Talent and Treasure to achieve God's plan for my life;
- God has given me free will as to how I use them;
- I am a steward of my life. God owns it if I am submitted to Him;
- It is only in God's plan that I find the real fulfilment I seek;
- I make my greatest impact when I hit the gold centre of God's plan for my life;
- God puts on my heart the things which make up the target for my life. He has spoken to me and continues to do so;
- I am vulnerable to certain Giants but I can overcome them by choosing to believe God's Word about me and by remembering how big my God is compared to any Giant;
- Giants will try either to stop me from starting, to slow my progress down, or to divert me along unproductive paths;
- If I am unwise I can be robbed of or just waste my 3 Ts;
- God's plan for my life is not all about me. It is about what God wants to do for others through me;
- I am never too old or too young to have dreams in God and to do something towards them;
- A dream without action is a daydream; and
- I can dream, dare, create, grow, and expand what God wants me to do so that I reach my full potential in Him and for Him, stand strong and soar high.

CONCLUSION

In these closing pages I would like to cover two areas which are very close to my heart and to the hearts of those involved with the Crosslink Transformation Network.

1. The workplace; and
2. The concept of taking spiritual responsibility.

THE WORKPLACE

If we try to love God with all our hearts, soul, and mind (the Greatest Commandment) we also need to try to outwork what Jesus said was the Second Greatest Commandment which is to love others as yourself. We also need to remember that a commandment is very different from a suggestion. A commandment as defined by the Merriam-Webster dictionary is "the act or power of commanding".

If as a Police Officer a more senior officer suggested to me to do something, then I was left with a choice to do it or not. However, if that same senior officer gave me an order and commanded me to do something then as they had greater authority than me my choice was over-ridden, and I was duty bound to do as ordered; as commanded. Commandments are commandments not suggestions. We have the Ten Commandments not the ten suggestions. Jesus knows what He is doing so we need to pray, ask, listen, hear, trust, and obey.

Remember Jesus said "All authority in Heaven and on earth has been given to me. Go…." If I am sufficiently surrendered to God, I recognise and joyfully accept and submit to His authority.

Not out of a forced sense of duty but out of recognition and acceptance of His love for me and the rest of humanity. Sold out to His goodness and mercy. We are therefore to Go and make disciples of all nations….

The workplace is somewhere we have prolonged contact with so many others who are not yet Christians and Ed Silvoso in his book *Transformation* said, "Change the marketplace and you can change the world." The marketplace is where many millions of people work; it's a workplace. It is somewhere we work and into which we can GO…. just as Jesus commanded us to. That takes me on to:

TAKING SPIRITUAL RESPONSIBILITY

Your Whats will help you to achieve some, by now, hopefully clearly defined things as the unique individual He has created you to be. Yet we all have a key part to play in the Great Commission to share the Good News of the Gospel message with as many as we can so that through Jesus they can be reconciled to our Heavenly Father.

Can I now commend you please to say to God that you gladly accept the Commission you are being given. And further to tell Him that you accept spiritual responsibility for the others He connects you with and in particular those who work where you work.

Spiritual responsibility means in this context "the state or fact of having a duty to deal with something".

Going back to my days as a uniformed Police Officer I had a duty to deal with crimes which I saw being committed and those who were committing them. Along with the uniform came the responsibility. The public would rightly expect me to intervene and deal with the crime and any offenders.

I had been given authority to do so. I could not walk by on the other side of the road ignoring a crime in progress due to the responsibility I had. Yes, it might have been much more convenient for me to walk on by but the responsibility I had needed to over-ride any inconvenience.

If we are to be obedient in this, we need to accept responsibility for those God brings across our path. Responsibility to share Jesus with others. By this I do not mean 'Bible bashing' people whether they want to hear or not. But I do mean we purposely try to build relationships with those we work with and positively take opportunities as they arise.

God wants you to partner with Him where you work and ask Him what He wants you to do there and to be obedient to follow what He says. I know some professions are against you sharing faith including some in the NHS who do not want you sharing your faith with patients. That doesn't mean you can't share your faith with colleagues in a sensitive and supportive way especially in their times of real need.

Do you remember the parable of the Good Samaritan in Luke 10:30-35. A man was attacked by robbers, stripped of his clothes, and beaten leaving him half dead. In that parable a priest and then a Levite saw him and passed by on the other side of the road. However, a Samaritan took pity on him, went to him, and bandaged his wounds.

Then he put the injured man on his donkey and took him to an inn where he paid for the man to be cared for. In short, he took personal responsibility for the injured man. He could have also walked by but didn't. Then Jesus asked the man He was speaking to, who was an expert in the law, which one of the three was a neighbour to the man. The expert replied, "The one who had mercy on him" Jesus told the expert in the law "Go and do likewise."

I believe this parable is being repeated now, day after day, in workplaces around the world. No, I am not saying people are being beaten up and left for dead in your workplace. But I am saying that there are many, many people who are hurting because of what others are doing to them not just in the workplace but in their home life as well. Many people live difficult painful lives at home and bring that hurt with them into their workplace even if they do not talk about it at work, the pain is still there.

The pain of broken relationships, physical and emotional abuse. Loneliness, bereavement, drug and alcohol abuse, grief, and many other things beside. Yet day by day others pass by on the other side of the office or the shop, the factory, the warehouse etc. God has given us the responsibility to Go.

I invite you to see your workplace as somewhere God has given you responsibility for and to partner with Him in what He wants you to do there. Ask Him and be brave and obedient enough to take responsibility. Deliberately take time and effort to build relationships with others in your workplace. See yourself as their Workplace Pastor. Yes, little old you standing up and stepping out. Even if you are the only Christian there, He is with you always.

Ed Silvoso's various books such as *Transformation*, *Anointed for Business*, *Ekklesia* etc give some fabulous examples of how individual Christians just like you and me can have great impact on companies and organisations by taking spiritual responsibility for their workplace. If you don't know where to start then start by going to your desk, counter, till, and claim it for God inviting Him to come into it and be Lord of it and ask Him what He wants you to do next.

One of the saddest things I have heard was two people from the same workplace meeting each other at a Christian meeting outside of work and each said to the other "I never realised you were also a Christian". Neither had influenced their workplace at all and neither had taken spiritual responsibility for where they worked. How sad. There was not even any aspiration to outwork the Great Commission.

When I heard this, I found myself asking whether they were Disciples or just Converts? How many people at their work might have already needed a listening ear? Who was a neighbour to their workplace colleagues?

FINALLY...

Time is one of your 3 Ts. Use it wisely to avoid regrets later in life.

In his "The length of a Good Life" video on YouTube, Canon J John picks up on Psalm 90:10 which indicates that our life span is 70 years or 80 if we have the strength.

He says that if we settle on 70 years we can turn each decade into one day of a 7-day week. As I am writing this, it is my Sunday afternoon. What day of the week is it for you? Use the sheet on the right to mark which day applies to you and where you fit at the top or bottom of the day depending on where you are in life.

Remember, Jesus died on His Thursday morning, and we all know people who have not made it until the end of their week. That is why I say, "Life is a privilege and not a right." You are alive now and so **your destiny** is now.

I encourage you to take that privilege and live it in the level of fulfilment which comes from finding and living in the centre of God's will. Be that Arrow in God's quiver.

A closing scripture is Philippians 3:12. (NKJV) – *"Not that I have already attained, or am perfected: but I press on, that I may lay hold of that for which Christ Jesus has also laid hold of me"*.

Please press on now, do not be dissuaded or distracted. Find out what it is that God wants you to lay hold of and for which He has laid hold of you".

The purpose of encouraging you earlier to break each action plan, for your Whats, down to the point where there is nothing stopping you from taking that very first small step is so that you now know what you have to do. It is only your will that can stop you from starting on an exciting journey. Start NOW. Don't give in to the Giant of procrastination. You have waited this long in your life to get to this point so don't wait any longer. Take that first step.

God bless you in finding and hitting the gold centre of your life targets and also your Life Mission.

WHAT DAY OF THE WEEK IS IT FOR YOU?

Age Day	0 – 9 MON	10 – 19 TUES	20 – 29 WEDS	30 – 39 THURS	40 – 49 FRI	50 – 59 SAT	60 – 70+ SUN
Time AM PM							

What has God put the unique me on this earth now to achieve?

GATEway TO DESTINY

Giants
Arrows
Targets
Eagles

"Behold, the Lord thy God hath set the land before thee; go up and possess it, as the Lord God of thy fathers hath said unto thee; fear not, neither be discouraged."

(Deuteronomy 1:21)

Printed in Great Britain
by Amazon